The Book of Spinjitzu

*"THE ROAD IS LONG AND WINDING,
AND YOU ARE ONLY AT THE BEGINNING."*

I have studied Spinjitzu all my life, but there will always be more to learn. My father, the First Spinjitzu Master, taught me the ways of Spinjitzu and the wonders of Ninjago — the world he created. Since I was a boy, I have recorded these lessons so that I may teach others. Parts of this book are from journals I kept as a child and young man (yes, I was young once!). I wrote other parts as I have continued my studies. Now, late in my journey through life, I have added more notes to these pages . . .

To possess *The Book of Spinjitzu* is to bear a great responsibility. The information it contains is to be used wisely, and only for good. It is my hope that you, my reader, will let the power of Spinjitzu unlock the True Potential within you and become one of Ninjago Island's great champions. Someday I will be gone, and this book is my legacy . . . as are you.

WITHDRAWN

 — Master Wu

THE PHILOSOPHY OF SPINJITZU

"NOT ALL LESSONS ARE ABOUT FIGHTING."

My father's first lesson was this: Spinjitzu is more than an ancient martial art of punches, kicks, flips, and throws. It is a philosophy of living that takes a lifetime's journey to acquire. As a boy, my greatest desire was for Father to teach my older brother, Garmadon, and me how to defeat the forces of evil. Though I would indeed learn how to do this, I would go on to learn so much more.

BALANCE

Spinjitzu is about balance. Not just how a ninja stands as she fights, but also how she balances the Light and Darkness (good and bad) within herself and the world around her.

ROTATION

Spinjitzu is also the art of rotation, which is key to how a ninja moves. It teaches flexibility during battle and in life, which is full of change. Rotation is a source of strength. It adds force and momentum to blows. Once mastered, rotation helps a ninja create an elemental tornado. It also comes in handy while dancing!

Spinjitzu mirrors the qualities of its students. Only a true Spinjitzu Master knows that human potential goes far beyond what most people can imagine. Spinjitzu is a quest for total perfection. It may not be reached, but there is value in trying.

I was very young when my father explained that Garmadon and I needed to uphold and pass on the legacy of Spinjitzu. Taking on such responsibility as a boy was daunting. From the beginning, I took my studies very seriously. I did not want to let my father down.

MASTER CLASS

"TO BECOME A TRUE NINJA, YOU MUST BE ABLE TO SEE WHAT OTHERS DO NOT SEE."

One day, I will become a ninja! Father says being a ninja is one of the best things you can be. A ninja is honorable and strong. A ninja never quits and never leaves a friend behind. A ninja helps those who need it, and keeps dark forces from spreading evil. Look out, dark forces — soon I will be coming for you! (As long as the dark forces aren't too dark . . . I still leave the light on when I go to sleep.)

Garmadon and I enjoy listening to Father's stories from long before time had a name. I want to grow up to be just like my father. He is so calm and peaceful — except when Garmadon and I fight. "Brothers should not fight," Father says.

Even if I am never to be the master that he is, I know I will learn many things. As Father likes to say, "The journey is more important than the destination." I am excited to see how far I can travel on my journey.

TRAINING DAYS

"A NINJA NEVER QUITS!"

Training is hard. I didn't think it would be like this. When the training sessions are over, I'm so tired I can barely lift my chopsticks!

Before sunrise, Garmadon and I stretch our arms, legs, necks, shoulders, backs, and even our eyes and ears. Father says stretching loosens the body and mind for the challenges ahead.

NECK STRETCHES   LEG STRETCHES

????

Then we run the training course Father has built. Something always throws, trips, or smashes us! Father just drinks his tea and says, "Fail," every time we fall. Then we do it all over again.

Next, Father leads us through Spinjitzu movements. We have learned hundreds of moves, but it seems there are thousands more. Sometimes I want to give up, but then I remember, "A ninja never quits." (Although sometimes a ninja REALLY wants to!)

The Great Devourer took my brother away from me.

Yesterday, something scary happened. During our training exercises, my katana was knocked over the monastery wall. Garmadon went to bring it back, but when he reached for it, he was bitten by a strange snake. Father and I were very worried, for we could tell a great evil had found its way into my brother's heart. The snake's venom could turn the purest of things wicked . . .

FINDING YOUR TRUE POTENTIAL

"SPINJITZU IS INSIDE EACH AND EVERY ONE OF US. BUT IT WILL ONLY BE UNLOCKED WHEN THE KEY IS READY TO BE FOUND."

Over the last few years, Garmadon and I have made great progress in our study of Spinjitzu. Father says that to reach a higher level of mastery, we must unlock our True Potential. In each of us, there are obstacles and worries that keep us from true greatness. It is only when we conquer those obstacles that our hearts will be free and our True Potential — our own personal elemental power or skill — will be unlocked. Then we can achieve higher goals and truly master Spinjitzu.

DOUBT

FAILING

EMBARRASSMENT

Me (trying to be brave)

Fear often prevents ninja-in-training from taking the next step forward. I wonder what my greatest fear is? Doubt? Failure?

Father said True Potential unlocks the power of Elemental Masters. What can I do to unlock my True Potential? What is my True Potential? Which element will I be connected to? Fire, Ice, Lightning, Earth? Am I even an Elemental Master? How will I be able to help Father protect our world from evil? I hope the future holds the answers . . .

KNOWN ELEMENTAL MASTERS:

Pale Man – Light
Griffin Turner – Speed
Skylor – Amber
Bolobo – Nature
Karlof – Metal

Gravis – Gravity
Neuro – Mind
Ash – Smoke
Jacob – Sound
Camille – Form
Tox – Poison

Kai – Fire
Cole – Earth
Zane – Ice
Jay – Lightning
Nya – Water

Me, Elemental Master of ????

THE JOURNEY TO MASTERY

"ONLY A TRUE SPINJITZU MASTER KNOWS THAT THE HUMAN POTENTIAL EXCEEDS WHAT WE DARE TO IMAGINE."

Every morning, I ask Father, "Have we reached our True Potential yet?" But he always answers, "When you do, you will be the first to know!" But how? There is so much I still don't understand. I must work hard, and study even harder.

Garmadon is becoming less interested in unlocking his True Potential. He does not follow instructions and will not practice by himself. He has changed. A growing Darkness within him is pushing him away from the path our father hoped he would take.

I train each day. I wish to harness not just my physical potential with Spinjitzu movements, but also my mental potential by studying their meaning. Everything in Spinjitzu is done for a reason, and every movement and thought has a purpose. These combinations are too many to count, but by understanding them all I may someday master Spinjitzu.

"Life is but a series of small steps toward your ultimate goal," Father likes to say. But I must admit, on many days, it feels as if we are walking backward!

SPINJITZU IN EVERYDAY LIFE

"SPINJITZU IS AS MUCH A PART OF EVERYTHING YOU DO AS BREATHING."

Father says many Spinjitzu movements involve Rotation, or turning. The Spinjitzu tornado is one of these movements. Father challenged us to find examples of Rotations in everyday life. Here are some:

We stir tea in the teapot to dissolve sugar in it.

Don't stir too hard, or the tea will spill!

We turn around to speak to someone behind us.

Pottery wheels rotate so we can make pots and vases.

It's wise to talk to only one person at a time.

By spinning a potter's wheel, we can create true pieces of art.

How will this training help me create my first Spinjitzu tornado? I must meditate on that and practice harder, for when I use Spinjitzu in battle, my moves should be quick and precise. Father assures me that stirring my tea properly is an excellent start.

MY FIRST SPINJITZU TORNADO

Today, Garmadon and I created our first Spinjitzu tornadoes! It was AMAZING!

Father sent us to the village to fetch tea. While we were there, bullies confronted us and tried to take the tea. Instantly, we put our training to use. The next thing we knew, we were in the center of whirlwinds that seemed strong enough to blow our enemies halfway to the Lost City of OUROBORUS!

The Spinjitzu tornado is one of the most important moves to master, and being able to perform one is a huge step forward.

"A THOUSAND-MILE JOURNEY BEGINS WITH THE FIRST STEP."

We must use precise motions to create the Spinjitzu tornado, which acts as a shield of energy. It protects the ninja, and it can also create devastating attacks. This is how I begin my Spinjitzu tornado:

1. I shout "NINJA-GO!" — this helps me concentrate and attain inner balance.

2. I begin a series of precise movements to build up momentum. Momentum increases as I begin to rotate. It builds into one balanced motion, almost a dance.

3. Once I achieve perfect balance, an unstoppable whirl of energy surrounds me.

4. I maintain the pace without losing force. At first, I feel a bit dizzy . . .

5. . . . but I've created a Spinjitzu tornado! Now each of my blows will be equally strong. Then I slow down, concentrate, and do it all over again. Practice makes perfect!

THE PROPHECY OF THE GREEN NINJA

"ONE NINJA WILL RISE ABOVE THE OTHERS . . ."

What's <u>my</u> destiny? Is my life's mission to become the Green Ninja? Or maybe it will be to <u>find</u> the Green Ninja and protect <u>him</u> (or her)??

"One ninja will rise above the others and become the Green Ninja — the ninja destined to defeat the Dark Lord." So says the Prophecy of the Green Ninja. Since the day my father first told me of this prophecy, I haven't been able to stop thinking about it.

The Green Ninja is the most powerful of <u>all</u> the ninja. It is said he will be revealed only when the Four Golden Weapons of Spinjitzu are laid out before him. It is also said that the weapons will recognize him. I wonder what that means? Will they say, "Hello, Green Ninja?" Somehow, I do not think so.

The Dark Lord is the Overlord — the eternal, indestructible enemy of all things good. He is a being born of pure darkness who was created when the first shadow fell, after my father formed the world of Ninjago with the Golden Weapons.

As it turns out, the Golden Weapons glow green in the presence of the Green Ninja.

Once we find the Green Ninja, we must protect him or her, as one day he or she will save us all. The Overlord's Dark Forces will want to keep the Green Ninja from mastering his powers, and they will stop at nothing to accomplish their goal.

THE DARK SIDE OF SPINJITZU

"SPINJITZU IS A SWORD WITH TWO BLADES."

Father says Spinjitzu, if not performed exactly right, can cause great harm. I learned that lesson today. During sparring, I rotated my hips too much while executing a Kick of the Mantis, and I accidentally sent Garmadon flying through a support beam. The entire roof almost came down on him!

Afterward, Garmadon lashed out at me with a kind of anger I had never seen before. He was so furious, he didn't use Spinjitzu correctly. And he nearly destroyed the entire monastery before Father calmed him down!

These days, it seems there is almost as much Darkness in Garmadon as Light, and nothing Father tries can reverse it. Now my brother is undergoing different training — training my father hopes will return him to the right track. Father says using Spinjitzu for evil purposes could affect the balance between good and evil, and that whoever gives in to that temptation could destroy the world.

I will not let that happen to me.

THE SCROLL OF FORBIDDEN SPINJITZU

"SOME SECRETS ARE BEST LEFT HIDDEN IN THE SHADOWS."

One day, we were browsing Father's library, hoping to find a cookbook to replace Father's usual "plain noodles." When Garmadon pulled out a book called *The Art of Broth*, a scroll of black paper fell from its pages. He picked it up and said it felt hot.

He wanted to read it. I sensed we should not. Garmadon started to unroll the scroll when Father raced in and snatched it. He told us never to touch "the Scroll of Forbidden Spinjitzu." Then he ordered us to leave.

The next day, Garmadon returned to the library. He said the scroll was "calling" him. I should have told Father, but instead I followed my brother. The scroll wasn't there, much to Garmadon's frustration . . . and my relief.

Sometimes I wake at night and find Garmadon is missing from the bed next to mine. I imagine he is looking for the scroll. I cannot imagine what dark secrets it contains. A long-forgotten phrase that will turn the sun cold? A chant that will raise the spirits of the departed? A great tea recipe?

As I suspected, Garmadon was still looking for the scroll . . . and he eventually found it. We couldn't believe what was inside it! Here are the dark secrets it revealed:

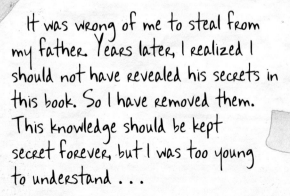

It was wrong of me to steal from my father. Years later, I realized I should not have revealed his secrets in this book. So I have removed them. This knowledge should be kept secret forever, but I was too young to understand . . .

TWO BROTHERS, TWO PATHS

"LEARN, PRACTICE, AND APPLY YOUR TRAINING. THIS IS THE ONLY WAY TO DISCOVER YOUR PATH."

As part of our training, Father has sent Garmadon and me out to explore the world to experience the wonders he created, meet its people, and learn some of the challenges we will face as its defenders. "You cannot protect what you do not understand," he says.

I hope our trip will bring Garmadon and me closer together. I miss my brother. I can see in his eyes that he is fighting the growing evil coursing through his veins. Perhaps our journey will slow, or even stop, the progress of that evil. I hope so.

I don't know where destiny will lead us, but we have made a list of destinations. We hope to have a new adventure in each of these places.

1. A trip to the Corridor of Elders to see the statues of Ninjago Island's heroes. (Remember to pack climbing gear.)

2. A hike to the top of the Wailing Alps to admire the view. (Don't forget the earplugs!)

3. Cross-country racing with Treehorns in the Birchwood Forest. (Garmadon swears they exist!)

4. A seafood dinner in the City of Stiix. (I love regional cuisine.)

5. A trip to the Holy City of Domu. (Father has recommended quite a few good reads from the city's famous library.)

We were young and innocent, but also brave and eager. Though we set out on the same journey, we would soon arrive on very different paths.

THE GOLDEN WEAPONS OF SPINJITZU

"THE GOLDEN WEAPONS ARE THE FOUR PILLARS ON WHICH THE WORLD OF NINJAGO STANDS."

It has been many years since I've written in my journal. Now I must continue my work and keep the promise I made to my father. I miss him dearly.

Father has gone to his eternal rest, leaving Garmadon and me to safeguard the Golden Weapons of Spinjitzu. It was not long before my brother gave in to the evil urges inside him. He tried to take the weapons. He was determined to use them and Spinjitzu to bend the world of Ninjago to his will. But I could not allow it.

My brother, Lord Garmadon

We fought, brother against brother. I used everything I had learned about Spinjitzu and all the energy within me to stop Garmadon. I prevailed. When our battle ended . . . I had banished my brother into the darkness of the Underworld, whence no one has ever returned.

The Golden Weapons are the most powerful weapons of creation known to man. The safety of our world is in my hands, so I must put aside grieving over the loss of my brother and do my best to protect the weapons.

Each weapon lets the user channel the power of its element.

When a skilled Master of Spinjitzu wields these weapons, they can create amazing machines. Many years later, my ninja team found this power extremely useful in battles with the Serpentine tribes.

The Scythe of Quakes grants power over the earth. It can cut the hardest stone, bring about earthquakes, and create deep cracks in the ground.

The Sword of Fire grants the user control over flames and heat. True to its name, it can become a blade of flame and project firebolts.

The Shurikens of Ice are bladed throwing stars that freeze whatever they touch. They can project beams of ice.

The Nunchuks of Lightning are a short chain connecting two dragon-headed batons. When a ninja swings them rapidly, they create energy storms and shoot lightning bolts.

THE TRUST FACTOR

"A NINJA TRUSTS FEW, BUT TRUSTS THEM COMPLETELY."

My duties as protector of the Realm of Ninjago are so great that I cannot spend every moment with the Golden Weapons of Spinjitzu. And yet, it is only a matter of time before the forces of Darkness try to take the weapons by force. I know that, and I fear that time will come sooner than I expect.

Skulkins in the service of my evil brother . . .

Therefore, I have hidden the weapons in separate locations and posted special guardians to protect them. Should anything happen to me, I have created a map to the weapons and given it to a trusted friend, Ray, and his wife, Maya.

Father said to know someone well before trusting them. A ninja decides whether to trust someone not on the basis of their words, which can be false, but on their actions. Actions, Father felt, revealed if a person was good or not.

Ray's and Maya's actions have proved them to be good, honorable people who care for others, and for the world of Ninjago.

(I also like their children very much. Kai and Nya are capable of great things. I look forward to our paths crossing again in the future.)

Future heroes!

After our paths crossed once more . . .

THE NINJA OF TOMORROW

"THE PAST IS THE PAST, BUT THERE IS ALWAYS THE FUTURE."

In the years between journal entries, I tried a little teaching, grew a very impressive beard, and devoted many hours to study.

While meditating yesterday, Eventuali-tea showed me a vision of the future that revealed my brother returning from the Underworld! The world of Ninjago is in terrible peril. I am afraid I might not be able to protect it on my own.

MY READING LIST

1. Mastering Your Bamboo Staff: Attacks and Defense
2. Spinjitzu Tornado Techniques
3. Tasty Tea Recipes: An Ancient Handbook
4. Guide to the Serpentine Tribes
5. Mustache Maintenance for Beginners
6. The Art of the Silent Fist
7. Legends of the Temple of Fortitude

FIG. I.

SPIRIT BUSH. *BOSCUS SPIRITUM.*
ONLY FOUND IN THE CLEARING NORTH
of the FOREST of TRANQUILITY.

But I am sworn to uphold my father's legacy. The time has come to seek help, to find four chosen ones to become ninja who can wield the Golden Weapons in the fight against my brother. The new heroes could be anywhere, but I have some ideas about where to begin my quest. I must leave the monastery and begin my search immediately . . .

THE CHOSEN ONES

"WE MUST SHARE OUR WISDOM WITH THOSE WHO COME AFTER US."

After weeks of searching, I have found the four young people destined to become the protectors of the Four Golden Weapons of Spinjitzu. Each ninja-in-training has great potential waiting to be unlocked. It is my responsibility to help them become what they are meant to be.

Cole tested himself by climbing one of the tallest mountains on Ninjago Island, and I met him at the peak. Something was troubling Cole, and he was fighting it on the inside. Cole always wants to be the best at everything. When I told him about the potential I saw in him, he was eager to study to become a master of Spinjitzu.

Jay was testing his latest invention, mechanical wings, when he crashed in front of me on a rooftop. He is energetic, funny, and tends to hide his insecurities behind jokes. But he doesn't hide his desire to help others. Jay will become the Lightning Ninja.

I found Zane at the bottom of a frozen pond, trying to see how long he could hold his breath. (The fish around him were eager to learn the answer, too!) Quiet, cool, and logical, the aspiring Ice Ninja knows little of his past, but I see a bright future in him.

Zane could hold his breath longer than anyone suspected, but we wouldn't learn why for a long time!

Kai joined the team as the future Fire Ninja. Kai is the son of my dear friends Ray and Maya. We met again when Kai and his sister, Nya, fought off Skulkin Raiders sent by Lord Garmadon to retrieve the map to the Golden Weapons hidden in their father's forge.

After being kidnapped and rescued, Nya joined her brother to train at the monastery.

Now I must train these very different personalities in the art of Spinjitzu. It is my duty to help them master their abilities and mold them into a team. They can only protect the world of Ninjago from the coming storm if they work together.

TEAM SPIRIT

"THE BEST WAY TO DEFEAT AN ENEMY IS TO MAKE HIM YOUR FRIEND."

Cole, Jay, Kai, and Zane have begun training together. They need to learn how to wield their weapons and become skilled with Spinjitzu techniques. It is taking some time for Kai to fit in. He and Cole are especially competitive and rarely see eye to eye.

Sipping tea and saying "Fail" as they struggle through training, like my father did for Garmadon and me, makes me smile. (But only on the inside! It is too soon to show the ninja my sense of humor.)

The ninja must not see each other as rivals or enemies. Every team member must trust that the team is there for him, no matter the situation. Trust only comes with gradually getting to know the true heart of another.

Today Jay told me he wants his weapon to look like the one in his favorite video game!

My ninja understand the great responsibility that rests on their shoulders. Protecting the Ninjago Realm from evil requires skills, determination, and power. What they still need to discover is that each of them is an Elemental Master. If all goes well, soon they will unlock their True Potential.

The ninja remind me of me when I was younger — excited, eager, and sorely in need of discipline!

SPINJITZU TRAINING PROGRAM

"EVEN LESSONS LEARNED THE HARD WAY ARE LESSONS LEARNED."

I have taught many ninja over the years. At first, it was not easy, and I made mistakes. But over time, I found the ideal combination of exercises and moves for my Spinjitzu training routine. Some of those are described here.

LEG WARM UP

1. Taking a wide stance, lunge to the left, and then Right.
2. Lift one leg straight up in front without bending your back. Repeat with the other leg.
3. Holding on to something for balance, lift one leg behind you as high as you can. Repeat with the other leg.
4. Lift and swing one leg from side to side. Repeat with the other leg.

Balance is key in every Spinjitzu movement. Finding balance is everything!

IMPORTANT: Don't try this at home! These moves are best learned under the guidance of a trained Spinjitzu Master.

ARM WARM-UP
Swing arms forward, then backward, and finally one arm forward and the other backward.

Repeat each exercise ten times.

HEAD WARM-UP
1. Turn head slowly to the left as far as you can, and then to the right.
2. Bring head down toward chest, and then tip it back as far as you can.

HIP WARM-UP
1. Plant your feet firmly on the ground, arms stretched out at shoulder height.
2. Twist body from side to side as if you are wringing out a wet cloth.
3. Repeat the movement with hands on hips.

At first, my students said the exercises were a waste of time. But after a week's training, they found they were a lot more flexible, and they quickly changed their minds!

A strong defense is the best attack. Spinjitzu teaches us to be peaceful. These stances — if properly performed — may be enough to make your opponent surrender.

PINCHED CRAB

BALANCE!!!

1. Stand with your feet apart, facing outward.

2. Bend legs at knees.

3. Raise arms to shoulder height.

4. Cup hands like crab pincers.

Father's original version called for feet to face forward. After seeing many students stumble and trip, I altered this stance and had my students face their feet outward to achieve better balance.

SWOOPING CRANE

An excellent move for distracting opponents!

1. Hold arms out to sides, palms down.

2. Bend upper body, arching back.

3. Bring head up slowly.

TIGER CLAW

1. Stand with legs bent at knees, feet shoulder-width apart.

2. Bend arms and raise them at elbows. Spread fingers and bend them like cat claws.

3. Lunge upper body forward and down, with hands out in front.

CURIOUS DRAGON

Roar loudly to intimidate your opponent!

1. Stand with feet together, facing forward.

2. Raise arms above head, bring hands together with fingers facing forward.

3. Thrust neck forward and lean head to one side, as though puzzled.

STINGING WASP

This is a good attack position, but it's also good for dodging, as you can leap to either side or back.

1. Bend legs at knees, and keep feet together.

2. Lean upper body forward over knees.

3. Extend arms in front, palms together.

The key to mastering the following sequences is maintaining <u>balance</u> while spinning.

IMPORTANT: Do not attempt to perform these exercises without the supervision of an experienced Spinjitzu Master!

SIDE ROUNDHOUSE SWING

1. Stand with knees bent, one foot in front of the other.

2. Turn at waist.

3. Quickly turn back, bringing back foot up and around. Then drive rear knee toward target.

Nya amazed the other ninja with her skill in this sequence!

SEESAW

1. TEAMWORK: Two teammates stand back to back and interlock elbows.

2. Ninja A bends forward. Ninja B, on ninja A's back, kicks legs straight out to strike.

3. Ninja B bends forward. Ninja A, on ninja B's back, kicks legs straight out in the opposite direction.

Kai and Jay were super excited about practicing this move.

GRASSHOPPER JUMP

Zane loved practicing this sequence on grassy meadows.

1. Bend knees and crouch as low to the ground as possible.

2. From crouch, extend arms above head, with hands in fists.

3. Spring straight up.

My students were in a hurry to learn more complicated moves than these ones. But afterward, they were surprised how often they still use these basic blocks and attacks!

TORNADO FIST ATTACK

1. Forward-punch the air, constantly rotating the shoulder joint. Hold back the other arm to harvest more energy.

2. The opposite arm repeats the move.

3. Deliver every punch with full force and speed, creating a wall of fists.

This powerful technique is to be used for defense only — to get the upper hand in battle when conflict is unavoidable.

1. DON'T begin training without stretching first!

I always keep bandages and ice packs nearby in case of injury.

2. DON'T begin a training session with a teammate unless you are sure the teammate is ready!

SUGGESTION: Start all training sessions by yelling, "Training begins now!"

3. DON'T end a training session with a teammate until you both agree the session is over.

SUGGESTION: End all training sessions by yelling, "Training is over!"

Show respect for your opponent. You need them to train with you another day.

4. DON'T be overconfident!

Always wear safety gear when practicing!

5. DON'T attempt a new move or use a new weapon until your teacher says you are ready!

Enjoy yourself! Remember that exercising should be fun, so don't overdo it.

6. DON'T leave behind a teammate who's struggling with an obstacle!

Four arms and four legs can overcome an obstacle twice as easily as two arms and two legs.

THE NINJA AND
THE GOLDEN WEAPONS

"A RAZOR-SHARP WEAPON IS AN EXTENSION OF A RAZOR-SHARP MIND."

Since my students found the map I had entrusted to Ray and used it to reclaim the Golden Weapons, I feel that I have been reunited with a piece of my past. It is good to see the weapons in use once more, for the good of Ninjago Island.

The ninja have been practicing with the Golden Weapons — with varying degrees of success.

Cole has learned how to slam the blade of the Scythe of Earthquakes into the ground to create tremors. However, he must come to understand that when practice is over, the Scythe should be set on the floor <u>very gently</u>. Otherwise, his teammates could be in for a seismic surprise, as Jay found out one night.

Zane has nearly perfected the use of the Shurikens of Ice. His aim still needs a little work, however. Since his practice sessions began, three of my best teapots have been shattered.

Jay's progress with the Nunchuks of Lightning has been rapid. At first, he kept getting tangled in the chain. But now he is skilled at using the weapon for both attack and defense. And during a blackout, Jay discovered he could use the Nunchucks as a power source for his video game system.

Kai took to the Sword of Fire as though he was born to wield it. (In fact, he was!) He has incinerated many of my training mannequins and developed a "wall of flame" defense shield to discourage would-be attackers.

NINJA TRANSPORT

"A NINJA IS ALWAYS WHERE HE NEEDS TO BE."

While meditating last night, I had a vision of advanced ninja machinery. I usually tell the ninja that their most powerful weapons are their bodies and minds, while robots and intricate machines are for samurai. However, the ninja of the future will need fast vehicles, for they will have to face challenges in the farthest reaches of Ninjago Island.

It's a good thing none of the ninja are prone to seasickness . . . or airsickness!

Destiny's Bounty

The first vehicle I envisioned, the *Destiny's Bounty*, actually exists. For many years, this flying ship belonged to the feared pirate, Captain Soto. When Soto was defeated, the wreck of *Destiny's Bounty* came to rest in the Sea of Sand. I wonder what it would take to renovate the ship so my students could use it?

I imagine Jay Riding a fast motorcycle capable of crossing any terrain, with Jay's elemental power of Lightning boosting its speed.

Desert Lightning

I saw a desert in my vision of this vehicle, but I don't know what that means. Will Jay find it there? Will it be built there? Time will tell . . .

Samurai Mech

I also dreamed of a massive Robotic suit that can fly. It had missiles, a giant katana, and a net for capturing enemies. The Robot Resembled a samurai, but I could not see who was piloting it. Very frustrating!

This vehicle would be perfect for undercover adventures, like a rescue mission. In my vision, this Raider came to my students through unexpected circumstances.

Ultra Stealth Raider

First I saw a blurred image of a vehicle abandoned in a dreadful place, with dark energy running through its mechanical veins. Then a ninja appeared in the cockpit, and his elemental power drove the darkness out of the machine. Now I see the Tumbler in great detail, but one very puzzling question remains . . . Who is the Titanium Ninja?

Titanium Ninja Tumbler

Looking back now, I feel foolish for not immediately figuring it out!

Jay Walker One

This vehicle came to me in a
few lightning-fast flashes. I saw
a scientist working in a modern lab, pieces
of machinery being assembled, a blue roadster speeding
through the streets of Ninjago City, and some greenish semitransparent creatures
(ghosts?!) being chased and swallowed by the vehicle. I'm sure I saw Jay behind the wheel.

I envisioned this jet constructed in secret in
the dark corridors of a mysterious place.
Although I have never been fond of vehicles,
I felt this one would help its pilot escape from
grave danger.

Boulder Blaster

Much later it turned out I was right:
Cole used the jet to break out of Master
Chen's underground noodle factory!

DRAGONS: LEGENDARY AND REAL

"A LEGEND CAN BE A TRUTH NO ONE HAS SEEN."

My students' dragons flew away today and have not returned. Perhaps they have flown to the Spirit Coves to shed their skin? If so, what will they be like when they return? Will they have transformed and combined into the super-powerful Ultra Dragon, as the legends predict?

Dragons remain mysterious, but I believe my father created those beautiful creatures for a reason. I do not know how or when they first came to the Ninjago Realm. I do not even know if the Spirit Coves actually exist, since no living person has proven that they have seen them.

A Master of Spinjitzu can be a dragon master. Can a man and a beast be perfect guardians of the world of Ninjago?

Years ago, I tasked four dragons — each related to one of the elements of creation — to guard the location of the Golden Weapons. When my students retrieved the weapons and their individual connections to the elements were revealed, the dragons and the ninja became linked. The dragons became an important form of transportation for the ninja. They also became powerful allies.

Dragons can travel to the Underworld. Is it possible for them to travel through other realms?

But there are also Elemental Dragons, pure beings of elemental energy that can be summoned after an Elemental Master has unlocked his or her True Potential. Much later, when masters have faced their greatest fear, they can summon their Elemental Dragon — which is a manifestation of their courage and ability to triumph over doubt.

Once the Elemental Masters bond with the dragons, they can harness the beasts' energy and power. I'm proud of my students, the Spinjitzu ninja in training, who managed to forge that bond.

THE UNLIKELIEST NINJA

"IT IS NOT THE SIZE OF THE NINJA IN THE FIGHT, IT'S THE SIZE OF THE FIGHT IN THE NINJA."

The newest, youngest, and smallest of my students certainly was the least expected. He is my nephew, Lloyd Garmadon.

Lloyd

Misako

Wu

Garmadon

My father, the First Spinjitzu Master

I have met Lloyd — Garmadon and Misako's son. The boy wanted to be a villain to make his father proud. Still, I felt there was good in him, which he sometimes cannot hide. I'm sure he gets that from his mother. Sometimes I think of him as the son I could have had.

Lloyd went on to free the long-imprisoned Serpentine tribes, hoping he could command them, but they turned on him.

Lloyd decided to be good rather than evil, and he had just begun his Spinjitzu training when he was recaptured by the Serpentine and forced to serve them. I feel Lloyd will be a very important member of the ninja team. I must rescue him, but I will need help from my brother . . .

What a surprise!

PROGRESS REPORT

"THERE COMES A TIME WHEN WE ALL MUST GROW."

My heart is bursting with pride! During their quest to recover the Four Fang Blades, my students overcame personal obstacles and reached their True Potential. Each found his elemental power within Spinjitzu. I wish my father could have been there to see it!

Zane learned of his true history and accepted it. He can control ice and create amazing objects out of it!

Sometimes he also makes the Destiny's Bounty very cold!

Jay stopped pretending and realized that he just needed to be himself. Now the Elemental Master of Lightning can project powerful bolts of electricity!

Jay still doubts himself from time to time . . . but Nya always helps him regain confidence.

Cole made peace with his father, who had wanted Cole to follow in his footsteps as a performer. Then Cole claimed his destined mantle as Elemental Master of Earth, able to control rock and soil.

Kai remained impatient, but he managed to unlock his True Potential when he understood the value of teamwork — and that his team's destiny is to protect Lloyd, the future Green Ninja. Now he controls the power of his element — Fire.

Nya has yet to unlock her potential. She still needs training, but she's working hard . . .

TRAINING THE GREEN NINJA

"NINJA SHARPENS NINJA!"

When I finally discovered that the prophesied Green Ninja was my nephew, Lloyd, I was overjoyed. Then I realized that the final battle between the Dark Lord and the Green Ninja will, in fact, be a battle between father and son! My heart is broken. Will the boy be up to the challenge? Will I be able to prepare him?

Lloyd must train with the team and unlock his True Potential. My skills as a teacher have never been more tested. My ninja and I will do our best to make the Green Ninja ready to face his destiny!

LLOYD'S DAILY
TRAINING SCHEDULE

5:00 a.m.: Wake up

5:15 a.m.: Breakfast

6:00 a.m.: Stretching, rotation, and balance exercises — supervised by Kai

8:00 a.m.: Endurance hike at top speed — with Zane

11:00 a.m.: Free running and ballet class (to develop agility) — with Cole

12:00 p.m.: Lunch (with the team)

1:00 p.m.: Scroll and book study — with me

3:15 p.m.: Rooster chasing (to develop speed and reflexes), plus more spinning exercises

6:00 p.m.: Sparring (assign an off-duty ninja to be a sparring partner)

6:30 p.m.: Dinner (with the team)

7:45 p.m.: Obstacle course (including more spinning and balance exercises) — supervised by Kai

9:00 p.m.: Recreation — with Jay

9:30 p.m.: Bedtime (assign Zane to read a bedtime story)

The Green Ninja should be totally committed to his Spinjitzu training, but he shouldn't train beyond his strength. You can derive satisfaction from broadening your possibilities.

Can I get him ready in time? Are we pushing him too hard?

When the time comes to fight the Darkness, I do hope Lloyd is properly trained in Spinjitzu, for our enemy is strong. Yet my heart aches at the thought that the evil we will be fighting is my brother, too. Destiny plays cruel tricks on us . . .

NEARLY HUMAN

"YOU CAN BE MADE OF METAL AND
STILL HAVE A GREAT HEART."

Zane is the embodiment of what can be achieved through the practice of Spinjitzu. During our recent struggle to keep the Fang Blades from the Serpentine, he has discovered he is a Nindroid. It was not easy for him to accept the truth about himself, but eventually he understood that everyone is unique and has their own undiscovered potential.

I had observed Zane long before I approached him. I knew he was one of a kind, just like the other ninja I wanted to recruit. The day we met, before I asked him to join the team, he was sitting at the bottom of a lake, testing his resistance. I realized he was ready to start his Spinjitzu training.

It does explain why he is so special!

After overcoming his initial shock at discovering he was a Nindroid, Zane noticed a memory switch in his blueprints, and located it in his chest. When he reactivated it, his memories returned. Dr. Julien built Zane and treated him like a son. Before Dr. Julien passed away, he turned off Zane's memory circuits to spare him the heartbreak he would feel.

But with his memories restored, Zane experienced that heartbreak, and felt stronger having done so. Zane is grateful to be a unique Nindroid that can feel and experience friendship. We have all been unspeakably grateful to have Zane as a friend!

Before one can master Spinjitzu, one must completely accept one's self. I am proud of Zane for unlocking his True Potential.

DANGER, DANGER EVERYWHERE

"LISTEN TO YOUR HEART BUT BE GUIDED BY REASON."

Over the years, my study of Spinjitzu has taught me never to underestimate anyone as a potential enemy. Here are some great examples of this.

The evil Nindroids, constructed by tech genius Cyrus Borg to serve the Overlord, can appear mindless and not much of a threat. However, they are tougher and more agile than humans. Yet Nindroids are unable to gain strength from friendship, and they are incapable of making sacrifices, which is where some of the Spinjitzu Masters' greatest strengths lie.

Even the Nindroid proved surprisingly tough . . . especially when teased about his size!

A Skulkin named KRAZI is another surprising enemy. With his jester's hat and foolish behavior, he might not seem dangerous. But Spinjitzu teaches us that unpredictable enemies are the most difficult to fight, and KRAZI is certainly unpredictable.

Spinjitzu's strength also comes from the mind — and reason always defeats madness! Great for overcoming an unpredictable enemy like this one!

Knowing your enemies' strengths and weaknesses, regardless of their size, is the key to finding a way to defeat them.

Monkey WRetch, the chief mechanic for Nadakhan's pirate crew, doesn't really look menacing, but a Spinjitzu Master should never judge by appearances. Monkey WRetch's strength is not the same as a WARRIOR'S, but as a brilliant engineer he has built many dangerous machines.

INNER STRENGTH

"FEAR CAN HOLD YOU BACK OR PUSH YOU FORWARD."

Spinjitzu shows us that, more than any Nindroid, Serpentine, or Overlord, fear is a ninja's greatest enemy because it holds us back from true greatness. I have taught my students that in order to become real masters they should start believing in themselves, face up to their fears, and trust what their heart is saying.

COMMON FEARS:

1. Flying
2. Speaking in front of an audience
3. Heights
4. Clowns
5. The dark
6. Failing
7. Spiders
8. Flowers
9. Oatmeal for breakfast
10. Dogs
11. Dentists (especially ones dressed as clowns)
12. Snakes

I spend much of the ninjas' training time dealing with fear. Often, I will surprise them with what scares them most. Some are making great progress, but Jay still has a tendency to scream and run to his room. He will learn — these things take time.

If ninja can face and understand their fears, those fears are less likely to interfere with the ninja accomplishing their goal. Remember to center yourself when confronted with what scares you most. Nobody is free from fear. Even I fear I will fail others, my father in particular. He may no longer be with me, but I still do not want to disappoint him.

A NINJA'S APPEARANCE

"YOUR ENEMY MAY JUDGE YOU ON YOUR APPEARANCE, BUT YOU MUST ALSO SHOW THEM WHERE THE REAL STRENGTH LIES — INSIDE OF YOU."

To best practice Spinjitzu, a ninja's typical clothing, or gi, should be simple, functional, and allow maximum movement. A hood lets the ninja see, but does not reveal the ninja's identity. Boot soles are padded so the ninja may move silently. And the gi's three belts make sure a ninja's pants don't fall down during a fight. (Embarrassment can be a powerful weapon in the hands of an enemy!)

A Spinjitzu ninja always fights fair!

During training, ninja wear special helmets, chest protectors, and other padding so they don't get injured.

These outfits emphasize a ninja's abilities in battle: the tenacity of Ice, the spontaneity of Fire, the speed of Lightning, and the strength of the Earth.

The rocks that orbit Cole when he is doing a Spinjitzu tornado never seem to block his vision.

The ninja occasionally wear armored suits for combat involving heavy weapons. These suits have reinforced shoulder plating, sheaths for weapons, and masks that cover only the lower part of the face.

When fighting, Cole keeps his wallet under his shoulder plate.

When not in uniform, the ninja dress as typical young people. That way, they don't draw attention to themselves. And they also seem to find it comfortable.

HIDING IN PLAIN SIGHT

"MAKE YOUR ENEMY SEE WHAT YOU WANT HIM TO SEE."

Ninja must not only be good fighters, they must also be clever. Many missions call for speed, stealth, and disguise. Camouflage is an art within the art of Spinjitzu.

I'm proud of my students, who have practiced Spinjitzu's art of disguise in many different ways. When Nadakhan's crew took over the Misfortune's Keep, the ninja boarded it disguised as pirates . . .

Obviously, this was before they perfected the art of disguise.

My students have also improvised disguises using materials they had at hand. They once cobbled together disguises as Stone Warriors to sneak into Lord Garmadon's camp when he was still on Dark Island.

Nya has proven quite skilled at all manners of disguise. She posed as a Kabuki performer to blend in with Master Chen's entourage. She also designed and built the DB X and equipped it with software that allowed it to change its appearance so the ninja could travel unnoticed.

TO WARM THE SOUL

"EVERY CUP OF TEA IS LIKE A JOURNEY IN ONE'S MIND."

When our world is in peril, a true Master of Spinjitzu takes no rest and fights until the agents of Darkness are pushed back. However, there are moments when one needs to stop, relax, regain strength, and reflect upon the world through meditation.

My preferred method of relaxation is making and drinking tea.

Tea making is an art, just like Spinjitzu. It requires concentration and patience. The temperature of the water is important, and the timing and technique used to steep the leaves and extract the flavor is crucial. I was amazed to discover how much I had learned about rotation from stirring my tea . . .

There are enough different kinds of tea to satisfy the most sublime tastes. Some even have magical qualities. There is the tea that can speed up the aging process, and the tea that helps one forget certain events (highly desirable, but rarely available). When made properly, some teas allow you to transport yourself across enormous distances and even between realms (a comfortable method of traveling for a Spinjitzu Master, I must admit). These all can be bought in Mystake's tea shop.

Mystake's tea shop

I have often dreamed of opening my own tea shop. I look forward to making my own blends and showing customers the delights and benefits of tea.

I've been told about a type of tea that helps its drinkers grow a mustache and beard. Who would need such tea?

EVERYONE HAS POTENTIAL

"THE ONLY CONSTANT IS CHANGE."

Spinjitzu teaches us to Recognize potential even in our enemies.
Someone who is our adversary today might become our friend
tomorrow. Life has proven many times that everyone deserves
a second chance.

Here are some examples:

When we met Lloyd, he was our enemy. Initially he allied with the
Serpentine, but when he discovered their evil nature, he joined the
ninja and me. He even sacrificed his youth to become the Green Ninja.

Lloyd's father, Garmadon, experienced several changes of heart. Initially, he was pure of spirit and a devoted student of Spinjitzu. But after the Great Devourer bit him, his spirit was poisoned, and he slowly became evil. Later, when his son was in peril, Garmadon returned to the side of good and gave his life to save the Realm of Ninjago.

Another example is my first Spinjitzu student, Morro. I suspected he might be the Green Ninja, but when we learned he was not, Morro couldn't accept it. He wanted to prove that I was wrong, so he left the temple and became my fierce enemy. Nevertheless, in the fullness of time, we discovered he wasn't entirely evil. He returned on the Day of the Departed to help the ninja and me.

Nothing remains the same forever. Change is a part of everything. A student of Spinjitzu must be open to change, and flexible enough to deal with it.

AIRJITZU

"SPINJITZU IS A TREE FROM WHICH MANY BRANCHES GROW."

All new martial arts can be traced back to Spinjitzu. The one created by Master Yang is a perfect example. Yang was a keen student of Spinjitzu. Who trained him, I don't know. But, like me, he was also extremely interested in the possibilities and powers of Spinjitzu. He carefully studied it and developed his own movement called Airjitzu.

Yang wrote the secrets of the martial arts discipline of Airjitzu on this ancient parchment. The scroll now resides in the Library of Domu.

Jay insists on calling Airjitzu "Cyclon-Do."

Users of Airjitzu create elemental tornados that allow them to fly for short periods of time.

Important: To maintain an Airjitzu tornado, keep legs tucked during flight.

Important: Be aware of weather conditions before forming a tornado!

Although many of his deeds were not glorious, Master Young will always be remembered and highly esteemed for developing Airjitzu. I am confident that there are other martial art forms related to Spinjitzu. As a student of Spinjitzu, I must continue documenting my father's work.

MUSCLE IN MIND

"YOU MUST TURN THEIR GREATEST STRENGTHS INTO THEIR GREATEST WEAKNESSES."

Spinjitzu teaches us that what may seem to be a weakness can be turned into a strength. Cole's story, after he had become a ghost, is the perfect illustration of this teaching.

Cole: Normal

Cole: Ghost

Cole found himself trapped inside Yang's Haunted Temple, the old Temple of Airjitzu, at sunrise. As the legends foretold, he was transformed into a ghost. He became depressed, believing that as a ghost, he could no longer be a part of the ninja team.

Nya suggested that rather than dwell on what he could not do, Cole should find other ways to help. Cole learned that he could possess materials and objects and even pass through walls. These abilities proved crucial in defeating both Morro and Nadakhan.

Even a small impediment can be used to one's advantage. Once I got the hiccups during a fight, and I used it to deceive my opponent. I faked an extra hiccup while sneakily delivering an unexpected blow!

When he returned to his human form, Cole unlocked a new elemental power — the Earth Punch — that he is now struggling to harness.

Fumbling speech in a time of crisis can also add to the time it takes to convey information . . . and help gain precious time before reinforcements arrive.

Never forget: A weakness is only a weakness if you let it make you weak.

DIFFERENT WARRIORS, DIFFERENT WAYS

"MANY ROADS MAY LEAD TO THE SAME DESTINATION."

Simple and light

The samurai and the ninja are a very different. The former rely on their extraordinary weapon skills; the latter derive strength from their bodies and minds.

Great warriors never miss an opportunity to learn and develop their skills. The samurai and the ninja can learn from each other. Spinjitzu encourages an endless quest for inspiration.

Flexible and stylish

Quiet and easy to clean

Helmet — elaborate, but makes vision difficult

Armor — protective, but restricts movement

Although the heavy armor never affected Nya's performance, I'm happy she has passed on her Samurai X legacy to someone else . . .

Samurai Sword — dangerous, but requires time and space to use

For a long time, Nya fought alongside the ninja as the mysterious Samurai X. She managed that role very well because she is an inventive engineer. It is difficult for her to follow the path of the Master of Water without the mechanized armor she had as Samurai X, but I am certain she will find her inner strength and confidence and become an excellent Spinjitzu ninja.

ONE ART, MANY MASTERS

"SPINJITZU REFLECTS OUR QUALITIES AND PASSIONS. OUR DIFFERENCES ARE SHOWN IN HOW WE MASTER SPINJITZU."

My father was full of secrets. He never told me whom he had trained before Garmadon and me. Over the years, I have trained a select few, but somehow others across Ninjago Island have learned Spinjitzu as well.

Note for the future: Assemble a list of all known Spinjitzu masters. Who are allies and who are enemies?

My brother was a great Spinjitzu master. Could he have taught Spinjitzu to others before he was banished to the Underworld? I trained Misako before she married Garmadon, and we grew close during that time.

Nadakhan was a powerful, evil djinn with the ability to grant wishes. His henchman, Doubloon, once studied Spinjitzu, but that was long before he became a thief. Caught stealing from the *Misfortune's Keep*, Nadakhan made him into a mute, two-faced pirate.

Word to the wise: Never, EVER steal from a djinn.

Once Doubloon became Nadakhan's thug, he used Spinjitzu tornadoes in combat. That made me incredibly sad. Spinjitzu is not for pirates and thieves.

LEARNING FROM MISTAKES

"DO NOT WISH, ACT. ONLY THIS WAY YOU CAN INFLUENCE THE PRESENT."

It is important to dream and have ambitions, but wishful thinking can lead to disaster. Our recent clash with a wish-granting djinn proved that I have not spent enough time teaching my students the dangers of wishful thinking. This mistake turned out to be a hard lesson for the ninja and me . . .

Nya and Delara looked almost exactly alike.

Nadakhan, the powerful evil djinn I have spoken of, escaped captivity from the Teapot of Tyrahn. He kidnapped Nya, intending to marry her. He wanted to return the soul of his lost love, Delara, to Nya's body. If he'd succeeded, it would have given Nadakhan unlimited wishes of his own and made him invincible.

78

Nadakhan was not a foe that could be easily defeated with kicks and punches. He would cunningly trick his opponents by granting them wishes that turned against them. My ninja and I failed to seek the cleverest way to prevail within Spinjitzu. Thus, we fell into the djinn's trap when we recklessly wished for things or abilities we couldn't have. Fortunately, thanks to Jay's last selfless wish, we were able to defeat Nadakhan at last.

Were it not for Jay, we would have been trapped in the Djinn Blade forever!

This clash with the djinn was a lesson learned the hard way. The art of Spinjitzu focuses on harnessing the present. Of course, dreaming is important, but wishful thinking gives you nothing in return. Therefore, we all should reflect upon these simple truths:

1. A Master of Spinjitzu is not a person of words, but a person of action.
2. Make your dreams come true through your actions.
3. Think twice before you act, or you could get into trouble.

STRONGER TOGETHER

"SEARCH FOR THE POWER WITHIN, AND THEN REALIZE
THE GREATNESS WITHIN EACH OTHER."

I wrote earlier of not underestimating your enemies. The same can be said for your friends. Spinjitzu makes it very clear that everyone has a skill. Your friends can help you reach your goals.

This Spinjitzu teaching was evident during the battle with Nadakhan. Jay felt that because he was the only ninja with a wish left, it was up to him alone to save the world of Ninjago. However, he had other allies who were more than willing to help him.

The one-legged Captain Soto was experienced in fighting pirates; Skylor had the unique ability to absorb the power of others; Echo Zane was a rusty machine programmed to protect those who cannot protect themselves; Ronin was a thief, but he was resourceful and crafty . . .

Never forget one of the most valuable Spinjitzu teachings: No ninja stands alone.

. . . and the cranky Ninjago City Police Commissioner was committed to doing the right thing.

Ronin

Jay knew their obvious flaws and weaknesses, but he was also able to see the great potential in each of them. By standing together, they made a formidable team that helped Jay free the ninja from the Djinn Blade.

ALL AROUND THE WORLD

Ninjago Island, the home of Spinjitzu, is a Remarkable place full of many wonders. It is a vast land, with mountains and seas, forests, deserts, villages, cities, temples, and caves. Many are significant to its history and lore. I have traveled far and wide and discovered how beautiful my father's creation really is. Some places are worth highlighting.

DARK ISLAND

The world of Ninjago originally consisted of one huge island. When the Overlord's Stone Army threatened to overwhelm the world with Darkness, my father split the island in half, and Dark Island became the Overlord's territory. The island sank to the seabed and remained underwater for years, only to resurface when Lord Garmadon reached it.

THE HOLY CITY OF DOMU

This ancient library holds many books and documents of great importance to the world of Ninjago, such as Master Yang's Scroll of Airjitzu.

Note to self: Must return overdue books!

On quiet days, I sometimes sneak off to the city's Mega Monster Amusement Park to ride the Spinning Teacups.

NINJAGO CITY

Ninjago City is Ninjago Island's largest metropolis, with everything a big city has to offer. Be sure to visit Mystake's excellent tea shop and see the magnificent Titanium Statue in the park.

JAMANAKAI VILLAGE

This peaceful village near the Mountains of Impossible Height was a key location of conflict during the Serpentine Wars. When it's not under attack, it's a popular holiday spot.

GLACIER BARRENS

The Tomb of the Hypnobrai tribe is located in this frozen mountain range. And the annual Ninjaball Runs through its peaks.

REMEMBERING OUR FATHERS

"IF WE NEVER LOOK TO THE PAST, WE CANNOT ENVISION THE FUTURE."

The Day of the Departed always makes me reflect on the past and the people close to my heart who are no more. I often think of my father. I would give anything to be able to see and talk to him again. And when I look at my nephew, Lloyd, I understand he must feel the same about his father . . .

I cannot say I have missed the evil spirits from Ninjago Island's history that the ghost of Master Yang summoned to fight us. But today, I am particularly grateful for the knowledge and skills I have learned from my father.

Kai and Nya relied on their knowledge of Spinjitzu when they faced Master Chen. They had learned how to take advantage of the enemy's weakness, and they realized Master Chen's weakness was overconfidence.

Cryptor fought Zane in Birchwood Forest. The ninja tricked the evil spirit into destroying the mannequin he had possessed with his own Techno-Blade and, without a body to house him, Cryptor's spirit fled.

I have told my students many times that the power of Spinjitzu also comes from friendship. Obviously, Jay learned this lesson — he teamed up with Ronin to fight Samukai and his skeletons at Ed and Edna's junkyard.

Kozu and a squad of Stone Warriors attacked the ninjas' friend Dareth, but he remembered the Helmet of Shadows. He used its powers to take command of the warriors and force them to destroy Kozu's mannequin . . . and their own.

Dareth fancies himself the "Brown Ninja." But he is no ninja, and he will never be one, unless someone teaches him. (And it will not be me, that I can promise you!)

Pythor teamed up with the spirits and nearly crushed Lloyd under the severed head of a giant statue. But with Misako's encouragement, Lloyd rallied the power of the Green Ninja to turn the tables.

The spirit of MORRO RETURNED to face me. BUT RATHER than fight me, he helped us defeat the ghosts. PERHAPS it was his way of making up for the past.

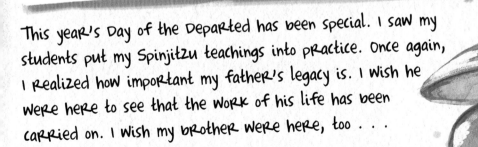

This year's Day of the Departed has been special. I saw my students put my Spinjitzu teachings into practice. Once again, I realized how important my father's legacy is. I wish he were here to see that the work of his life has been carried on. I wish my brother were here, too . . .

But I do not despair because I remember my history. Garmadon has returned to me when I thought him gone forever. Perhaps he will do so again. And I still have Lloyd. I can see so much of his father and grandfather in him!

AN ALLIANCE OF ELEMENTS

"A STRAW ALONE IS WEAK, BUT MANY WOVEN TOGETHER CAN BE AS STRONG AS STEEL."

"Ninja sharpens ninja," my father always said. And my old man was right. Now I am an old man myself. But the curious thing is that no matter how old we get, we keep forgetting and learning this again. A Spinjitzu ninja needs strong friendships and alliances, people you can trust, because one day, you will need to stand united against a common threat.

The original Elemental Masters were the First Spinjitzu Master's guardians. Most of these men and women were not Spinjitzu ninja, but skilled fighters to whom my father granted special elemental powers. The Elemental Alliance was born.

Generations later, my brother and I fought side by side with the Elemental Masters in the Serpentine Wars. After that, there was a time of peace. When the Hands of Time, Krux and Acronix, rebelled against us, the Elemental Alliance reunited to save the realm of Ninjago.

My friends, Ray and Maya (Kai and Nya's parents), used Chrono-Steel to forge special weapons — Time Blades that could absorb one's elemental power. Only with those unique weapons were Garmadon and I able to defeat the evil Time Twins.

There are four Time Blades:

- Forward Blade
- Reversal Blade
- Slow-Mo Blade
    - Pause Blade

When all four are put together, the Time Blades hold the power to time travel!

POWER CORRUPTS

"TIME IS THE THREAD THAT SEWS
THE FABRIC OF THE UNIVERSE TOGETHER."

Time can change villains into heroes, and heroes into villains. Our confrontation with Krux and Acronix proves this.

Power can corrupt anyone, even the most warmhearted among us. Krux and Acronix had the strongest powers of all of the members of the Elemental Alliance. Over time, they started to believe that their immense power entitled them to rule the realm of Ninjago.

End of the
Serpentine Wars

Krux and Acronix betray the Elemental Alliance and war breaks out.

Luckily, Garmadon and I foiled the brothers' plans. Knowing how dangerous the Time Blades could be — and that time was too great a power for anyone to control — we threw the weapons into a Time Vortex. We hoped they would be lost forever, but the Hands of Time leaped in after them and disappeared.

Acronix has arrived from the past. For him, it was a quick journey into a distant future. Now, facing me, an old man, he wanted to finish what we had started. This encounter did not go as well as I might have hoped. . . .

Spinjitzu teaches us that time is a river that flows only forward, but the Time Twins can speed ahead of the current, or travel back to a place already passed. Time travel is too dangerous. You change anything, you change everything . . .

Garmadon and I throw the Time Blades into a Time Vortex.

Ray and Maya forge the four Time Blades from Chrono-Steel

Krux and Acronix leap into the Time Vortex to Reclaim the Time Blades

We use the Time Blades to absorb the Hands of Time's powers

Note to self: Talk to Lloyd, it's very important that he . . .

FOCUS

"SHARPEN YOUR MIND AS WELL AS YOUR SPINJITZU."

The path to becoming a Spinjitzu Master is long and winding. The greatest challenge is to control oneself. A ninja must learn the art of concentration and move toward attaining inner balance.

Over time, I have come to recognize my students' greatest distractions. However, the aim is not to make them abandon these distractions, but rather to teach them to recognize situations in which the distractions shatter their inner peace.

Kai's primary distraction is anger. When he becomes upset, he loses his ability to help the team. He must stay focused on team goals.

Zane is a Nindroid, and people may not always understand his behavior. He focuses a lot on his sense of humor, so jokes sometimes make him lose his concentration.

Mistakes distract Cole. If he fails, the events play over and over in his mind, and he doesn't pay attention to what he's doing. And unless a ninja has a Time Blade, the past cannot be changed — the present is what matters.

Jay is often distracted by Nya, comics, and shiny things. Giving him duties crucial to our missions keeps him on track.

Lloyd's major distraction was his relationship with his father. He and Garmadon made peace before Garmadon sacrificed himself to save the world of Ninjago.

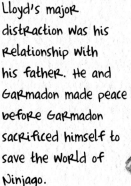

Nya is always distracted by Jay. To keep her focused, I remind her of her parents' focus on protecting my map to the Golden Weapons.

As my journey toward mastery of Spinjitzu continues, I strive to eliminate all distraction from my life. Well . . . a good pot of tea can still turn my head on occasion.

AMONG THE PURE-HEARTED, SPINJITZU ENDURES

"A WATCHFUL EYE NEVER SLEEPS."

If I have learned one thing in my years of studying Spinjitzu, it is that a ninja never comes to a point where he can say he has learned all that there is to know. True masters should always continue their quest, even when they are nearing the end of their days.

The Book of Spinjitzu is my legacy, which I will eventually pass on to my successors and which they will one day pass on to theirs — because the world of Ninjago will always need protectors. My father's teachings —and now mine — must live on.

If you are reading these words, it means that I am gone —
or that somehow this book has been lost.

Life is a great adventure. I have devoted mine to studying
the secrets of Spinjitzu, and I discovered that they can
be of value not only to ninja, but to all. The essence of
Spinjitzu lies in the ability to know and accept oneself,
because self-worth and inner balance are what helps each
of us weather adversity and gain confidence.

BE NINJA.

May your path be a long, healthy, and happy one. If my
teachings and reflections come in handy on your life's
journey, please do remember me sometimes — perhaps
over a nice cup of tea . . .